A Bountiful Silence

& Other Poems

A Bountiful Silence

& Other Poems by

John Muro

© 2025 John Muro. All rights reserved.
This material may not be reproduced in any form, published,
reprinted, recorded, performed, broadcast,
rewritten, or redistributed without
the explicit permission of John Muro.
All such actions are strictly prohibited by law.

Cover image "Tree Joy" by Kelly DuMar
First published in *Cool Beans Lit*

ISBN: 978-1-63980-984-4
Library of Congress Control Number: 2025944166

Kelsay Books
502 South 1040 East, A-119
American Fork, Utah 84003
Kelsaybooks.com

This book is dedicated to my children and grandchildren

Acknowledgments

Grateful acknowledgment to the literary journals in which these poems first appeared, sometimes in slightly modified versions.

Acumen: "Sea Drift"
Agapanthus: "Moths"
Ancient Paths: "Black Cap"
Ariel Chart: "While Sleeping," "Whistler's Nocturne in Black and Gold"
Aromatica Poetica: "Recess"
Blue Muse: "Sleeping Giant"
Clementine Unbound: "Garter Snake"
Connecticut Poetry Society: "Home Bound" (2025 Nutmeg Award Honorable Mention)
Connecticut River Review: "A Rural County in Connecticut"
Cool Beans Lit: "Cue the Barbizon," "The Quelling"
Cosmic Daffodil: "Latitudes," "Transformation"
Deal Jam: "A Want for Yellow," "Intrusion," "Odyssey," "Why I Choose to Waken First"
Delmarva Review: "Something More Than Winter (Weighs Upon Me)"
Eunoia Review: "Coastal Fog," "Tidal Ruin," "Weeding Near Dusk"
French Literary Review: "Blue Roofs," "Musicien Français (Claude Debussy)"
Freshwater Literary Journal: "A Winter's Night in New England," "Advent," "Backwash," "Morning: Piazza di Spagna," "Reclamation," "Scenic Road," "Windward"
Green Ink: "Restoration"
Green Silk: "Springtide"
The Hemlock: "A Nameless Loss," "Edinburgh Nocturne," "Lines for Anthony Louis," "Hope Repurposed," "My Muse Is Slow Arriving"

Hyacinth Review: "Cache," "House Finches," "Requital"
Literary Yard: "Abiding," "All In (on) Autumn," "Reconciliation"
Madison Journal of Literary Criticism: "After Listening to Copland's *Appalachian Spring*"
Mandarin Magazine: "Inheritance," "Reassessment"
MockingHeart Review: "Winter Offering"
MockingOwl Roost: "Awaiting Thrush," "Bermuda Nocturne," "Deconstruction," "Flood Plain," "Prelude," "The Migrants, 1957"
Moria: "Becoming," "Foretoken," "Renascence"
Mystic Owl: "Autumnal"
Neologism: "Al Fin del Dia," "Ash Wednesday," "In Search of the River," "Magpie"
New Square: "Bearded Irises," "Bonnard's Almond Tree in Blossom," "Capitulation," "Cedars," "In Low Light"
October Hill Magazine: "Consequential Light," "How Can You Mend a Broken Heart?" "Passiontide," "Unbidden"
The Orchards Poetry Journal: "Consecration" (Grantchester Award 2023 Recipient), "Moonbound"
Paddler Press: "The Connecticut in Winter"
Pato Journal: "Absolution," "Snow Leopard"
Penumbra: "Annalist"
Pilgrimmage Press: "With Apologies from the Atlantic"
Plentitudes: "Bequeathed"
Pluvia: "Evenfall," "Fortuity"
Poetica Review: "How Darkness Fell," "Untethered"
Raven's Perch: "Dissolution," "Earthly Blue Sublime," "Near Sachem's Head"
Rill & Grove Journal: "Mourning Dove," "Prologue," "What Once Was Luminous"
Sein und Werden: "How Shall We Return?" "Hummingbird," "Steps from Water"

Sky Island Journal: "A Bountiful Silence," "After the Fall (A Bruise Remains)," "Bloodgood Maple," "La Voglia di Sognare (The Desire to Dream)"
the tide rises, the tide falls: "Castaway"
Third Wednesday: "January Thaw," "Luce Divina," "Replenishment"
Valparaiso Poetry Review: "Beholden," "Goldfinch," "The Drowsing"
Wee Sparrow Poetry Press: "Dispersal" (Ekphrastic Contest Winner, December 2024), "Morning Idyll," "Scarcity"
Willawaw Journal: "Buttermilk Falls," "Early Morning: March"
Winged Moon: "The Evanescent"
Winged Penny Review: "Giving Way"

Contents

I. The Seasons

Prologue	19
Goldfinch	20
The Drowsing	21
Renascence	22
Morning Idyll	23
Early Morning: March	24
Advent	25
Absolution	26
Springtide	27
Requital	28
Bearded Irises	29
Becoming	30
Cache	31
Unbidden	32
Luce Divina	33
Near Sachem's Head	34
Deconstruction	35
In Search of the River	36
Foretoken	37
Autumnal	38
After Listening to Copland's *Appalachian Spring*	39
Bloodgood Maple	40
Latitudes	41
Odyssey	42
Cue the Barbizon	43
All In (on) Autumn	44
A Winter Offering	45
Replenishment	46
The Connecticut in Winter	47
January Thaw	48
Passiontide	49

Restoration	50
Something More Than Winter (Weighs Upon Me)	51
Transformation	52
Scarcity	53
Winter Night in New England	54

II. The Sea and Sky

A Bountiful Silence	57
The Evanescent	58
Moon Bound	59
Reconciliation	60
Fortuity	61
Sea Drift	62
La Voglia di Sognare (The Desire to Dream)	63
Home Bound	64
Consequential Light	65
A Nameless Loss	66
Fog	67
After the Fall (A Bruise Remains)	68
Dissolution	69
Beholden	70
Reassessment	71
Consecration	72
Castaway	73
Bermuda Nocturne	75
Al Fin del Dia	76
Flood Plain	77
Earthly Blue Sublime	78
Backwash	79
How Darkness Fell	80
The Quelling	81

With Apologies from the Atlantic	82
Steps from Water	83
Giving Way	84
Capitulation	85
In Low Light	86
Windward	87
Dispersal	88
Annalist	89
Coastal Fog	90
Reclamation	91
Tidal Ruin	92
Abiding	93

III. The Heart and Hands

A Rural County in Connecticut	97
The Blue Roofs, Rouen	98
Awaiting Thrush	99
Inheritance	100
Weeding Near Dusk	101
Prelude	103
How Shall We Return?	104
Bonnard's *Almond Tree in Blossom* (1947)	105
A Want for Yellow	106
Cedars	107
Sleeping Giant	108
Garter Snake	110
Hope Repurposed	111
Snow Leopard	112
Intrusion	113
Lines for Anthony Louis	114
The Migrants, 1957	116

Hummingbird	117
My Muse Is Slow Arriving	118
House Finches	119
What Once Was Luminous	120
Mourning Dove	122
How Can You Mend a Broken Heart? (1971)	123
Moths	124
Bequeathed	125
Recess	126
Magpie	128
Untethered	129
Buttermilk Falls	131
Ash Wednesday	132
Whistler's *Nocturne in Black and Gold* (1875)	133
While Sleeping	134
Morning: Piazza di Spagna	135
Scenic Road	136
Musicien Français (Claude Debussy)	137
Why I Choose to Waken First	138
Edinburgh Nocturne	140
Evenfall	141

*Heard melodies are sweet,
but those unheard are sweeter.*

—John Keats

I. The Seasons

And yet this end and this beginning are one.

—Wallace Stevens

Prologue

I waken to a day I cannot wait
to step into, pausing to hear
the weather and the countryside
calling, as the world brightens
in gradations of greenness and
undiluted blue and flows on
in the upswell of a morning
chorus of bird-song and a
strange alchemy of scents
teased from pine and pasture
that have been ferried by an
easy wind; no longer hurrying
towards tomorrow but slowing
my pace as I approach a copse
of birch and a soft rise in
the earth drawing into my
body the fertile beauty and
praiseworthy splendor of
this land, sensing, too, how
a place can surely shape a
person and wanting nothing
more than to be exiled here
with an expanding heart and
giving thanks for a life torn
open and in no need of mending.

Goldfinch

But for the downpour of yellow
that suddenly appeared without
sound where scrub pine stumbles
into a field of upturned stone and
high grass, there was little else
to hold me to that place. The bird's
brilliance resembled a shock of
summer that had somehow been
misplaced or discarded and left
to weather upon the lower branch,
brushed by a breeze I could not
feel nor hear, as it remained
motionless while rising and falling
like the flame inside some distant
lantern and so, with fewer hours
before me than behind, I paused,
grateful for the bird's abilities to
heal an aging heart on a day that
had been destined to forgetting
while, as sometimes happens,
the sky built itself back into
a bountiful nest of blue and
a cold sun glazed the skeletal
limbs of a leafless birch.

The Drowsing

Mere moments from dusk
and I can see how a near-
sighted sun's deftly passing
threads of straw-gold light
through the upper branches
of elms, as if the trunks'
staggered set of burls were
thimbles and the crowns
of the taller trees were
crumpled patches of brocade
that had to be gathered and
mended and then later dyed
with pigments of rose, courtly
bronze and indigo and, further
out, gaunt, leafless snags stand
forlorn besides the luminous
clay and brackish water of a
flood-lit marsh, appearing
like slight pieces of tinder
prepared to give themselves
up in brittle combustion, torches
flickering in calm air before
their trails of smoke are swept
skywards in cursive spirals
as silence steepens with the
weight of things lost and day-
light imperceptibly falls away.

Renascence

Certain that I have loved
as best I could and that I
have so little left to care for,
I gladly choose to give up
my heart and settle here,
on the woodland floor,
leaf-still with a life
of longing ended and
no memory of having fallen;
subsisting beneath the
nodding fonds of maiden-
head fern and the late
afternoon's pour of dappled
light, taking in the thrush's
exquisite offertory to oblivion
as the world exhausts itself
and unhurried day melts
into dusk much the way
I silently relinquish myself
in soft sacrifice, bidding
farewell and bleeding
out the last of color and
musty odors of decay,
while seasons arc then
bend to greening and
all falls back into the
fertile underside of earth.

Morning Idyll

—based on artwork by Zofia Katrinakova

It isn't mine to give, but
if it were, this would be
the type of day I'd offer
to you: a cloudless sky of
wayfarer blue slowly expanding
above the soundless sweep
of pasture and where green-
turning-gold-turning-back-
to-green leaves would be
set out, like tiny parasols,
above our ritual of leisure
and where we, set upon
chairs ghosting the field,
might pause to consider
and hear all that's been
unsaid: the mist long-lifted,
the hour's exquisite emptiness
and the softer fluency of
morning light flowing from
limb to limb while awaiting
the day's brighter splendor
and the first few notes of birdsong.

Early Morning: March

Past porchlight, the barn sleeps still,
huddled beneath the snow-bound
trees, while a worm moon of oriental
gold glazes fence-posts and the frozen ground.

Galvanized buckets laced with frost,
each to each dimly burns,
perhaps in search of a season lost
or one that's yet to come.

Now, though, is the hour of the halting heart
when time seems to slow and memories
and misgivings emerge, hover and then depart
like breaths outside the body.

Yet, at this cold hour, only darkness stirs
and settles like a burial shroud
across the earth; somewhere a bird's
futile call, neither soft nor loud,

spills to ear while weary eyes
know how day will end: a fervent blue
blissfully rising and meager clouds dyed
like peace flags unfurling in pastel hue.

Advent

Early spring and for a week or more
the sky has been fleeced with coastal
fog and faint drips of rain, and it seems

as if all the world has been bereft of
light and left to languish, but today
an urgent dawn is filling the space between

the hills and I'm wanting to buy the promise
that all will, at last, be made whole again
as the earth turns tender and giving and

we dream ourselves away beneath an
expanding sky of bucolic blue that buckles
the knees and staggers the heart, lending

a drowsy effect to every aptly named cloud—
cirrus and stratus and such—that extend across
the far horizon like an archipelago while

an orphan moon steals away, pale and
pitted, which is but another way of saying
that, in this world, nothing truly keeps,

including this brief moment of excruciating
splendor when steps slow and a sudden
trembling spreads across the chest—

though we try our mortal best to hold onto
those very things that will ultimately come
to haunt, bruise and abandon us.

Absolution

Not so much the spill
of coral and kiln-bright
orange—wind-brushed
and drifting away from me—
but the firebreak of damsel-
fly blue separating the
plane of the horizon from
the gravel bed of cloud
like a channel of snow-
melt I might rise towards
since it is good to leave
the edge of earth and
the frenetic rush of life
from time to time and ease
into these eddies and colder
pockets of calm, heart-
first and elbow-deep, where
I'd release my grief and
watch it diminish, then
dissolve, in descent, past
the luminescent flow, even
as there is less of me, and,
in that instant, I'd emerge
without burden, feral and
freshly replenished, free
of need and breathing in
the air's sweet blue water.

Springtide

Beside the pensive shore
pious flowers bow their heads
like hooded monks before
dawn devotions are said.

The wind, too, is spent
and draws still; even the birds
have abandoned air. All are content
to await the frenetic blur

of colors when eager stems of green
birth buds of beguiling-gold and Homeric-red
their craving for sun is deafening;
though petals, for now, are merely threads

that restrain the engorged blossoms
that stir and brightly burn
within, and the indulgent sun
they eagerly yearn for will soon turn

all from glory to an indelible grief,
and all that's living back to dust.
That which offers life a brief
reprieve also takes, as it must.

Requital

Poetry lifts the veil from the hidden beauty of the world.
—P B Shelley

Trudging uphill and weighted
with remorse when an April wind
rises, wails and bends my body
eastward, and so I put aside my
pack and pause to take in the
windswept world before me
and day's dalliance with dew,
a dissolving darkness and
the first meager light of morning
gradually glazing the hillsides
and low-lying fields, brightening
with the high-pitched scatter
of birdsong, the drawl of
slow water over stone, and
the blurred rustle of high
grass; soon over-come by
a still-bright moon, rose-
golding, and clouds in the
shape of furrows of upturned
earth like the month-away
bud-swell of blossoms
and then, heart-humbled,
taken by the unexpected
fragrance of the forest
floor and an urgent need
to do or say something
other than *thank you.*

Bearded Irises

—for Gail

On an afternoon adrift
and unmoored by wind,
I marvel at how these
irises betray my grief,
long languishing, ghostly
opulent and eerily forlorn,
as if April's alchemy is
drawing color from a
still-born earth even as
all eases into Eden.
Florid plumes, immersed
in mid-day light, arc in
anguish as their tongues
of lavender, fluent in
the language of whimsy,
belie their fragile forms,
even as their hovering
standards, like torn wings
fashioned from light, rise
in dappled flutter above
the ceaseless murmurings
of foraging bees.

Becoming

I stand here but am not here
adrift in summer air, a kind
of sleep, soundless, yet able
to hear the birds ambush darkness

with song and resurrect a world,
graciously given, where all is
unveiled in spectral splendor
while the heart expands with wonder:

a choir in each cough of wind;
the rupture of fragrance from
each swollen blossom that astonishes
and agitates the soul, and the way

random miracles gather, some
cupped in the well of my hand,
others, eye-distant, peripheral
enough to convince us to lean empty

and closer-in like a balsa tree—
more air than wood—its honey-
combed body traversing the under-
growth with lithesome ease and

a weightless want that propels it
beyond the threshold of a luminous
canopy, where, in supplication, its
lush sprawl greens a distant heaven.

Cache

A blood-shot moon's heat-
stunned and staggering
through slow-moving air,
and all things are held
close to ground, including
an asthmatic wind that barely
brushes quiet queues of
creeping pink and purple
phlox. Even tides appear
like ephemeral flares that
might ignite these tinder-
dry nibs of grass. That
we could, like the nuthatch
rifling through the feeder,
carry morsels of sunlight
and our mislaid hopes and
bury them deep inside the
crevices of trees or under
rutted scales of bark and
retrieve them when, deep
in winter, the world's all
knitted up and held, dead-
still, in quilted darkness.

Unbidden

I can hear morning's eager patter
tapping against my window as if there's
a clock to punch and dismissing outright
my want to spend this day in the quiet
retreat of miserly light, and knowing,
too, the fatigue that follows when I'd
be prone to dawdle and try to dream
myself back to sleep while the wind,
in a steady gait, leads me in a search
for beauty past pools of standing water
bordered by an understory of maiden-
head fern, lace hydrangea and viburnum;
and the intermittent swell and ruffle
of knee-high meadow-grass beyond
which, awestruck, I could stop to hear
the liturgical songs of birds greeting
the day from somewhere above
the garden with its alluring scents
of mint and sage and I find that my
want for seclusion has no currency
here and is but a lie I tell myself
in order to caretake an intractable
sorrow that arrived uninvited and
overstayed its welcome.

Luce Divina

A summer day of rain has ended and
the sun's dissolved into a mottled halo,
as otherworldly colors rupture and
expand in wisps that curl back into the
softer folds and backlit channels of cloud,
while birds, heart-plucked, fall to a
breathless silence as if in awe and the trees,
dew-kindled and unburdened by shadow,
dream of flight and seem to glisten as they
stretch upwards to gather, draw down and
don the last of this divine light that has
somehow been swept through an opening
at the bottom of heaven's door or else drifted,
like incense, though an unlatched window.

Near Sachem's Head

Summer is in free-fall
and the tree line's now
green-blue coppering
in late-day shadow,
while the last of day's
light is spread in saffron
scatter across the tides
that I'm watching advance
towards the shoreline,
only to retreat in a
shuddering ebb and,
as is their custom,
a smattering of ghostly
stars appear while the
whole of evening slips
into the sea and I try to
preserve this moment
with a want for nothing
beyond the silence of
ruin and the need to breathe
before I turn, distracted,
and take the footpath forged
from crumbled shells past
overgrown thickets,
long strands of salt-grass
and the boat-house listing
upon a salt-softened pier,
and there, further on,
adrift in darkness and
encompassed in calm,
the cluster of cottages
and our tiny windows
winking in golden light.

Deconstruction

Mud-rimmed pools of oil and grease,
the belching sound of brakes
too eagerly applied;
diesel motor's guttural sigh,
downshift creates
a putrid breeze
that's high-window and apple-bound.

Beneath plumes of acrid smoke, mandibles
freckled with rust
have misshapen and gouged
the land. Opaque clouds
of sour exhaust
blend with its manic clutch and chortle
birthing a blue abscess of sound.

Left wondering how best to mend
or even recall the lavish
orchard that once blossomed here;
or the bee-brushed, oriole-bright air
that seemed to combust
in orange dazzle and then dim
upon falling to misted ground.

In Search of the River

Seeing how the clouds convulse at first
then delicately unfurl in the manner of
ink taking to water, transforming into
something that has forsaken form and
assumed a second, more exquisite self
while here, closer to ground, I'm following
the long scar of a dry river bed where
the only sound comes from the lament
of birdsong somewhere beyond the
bruised earth and dusty air and the long
pause that follows—not silence exactly
but something approaching an exhaled
breath—is cradled by wind and carried
between this sluice of bedrock and banks
of fern, their golden fronds crinkled by
sun, and the boy inside me is now
guessing at the time when the canvas
of flowing water last served up sounds
and carried a weightless sky downstream
past the understory of broken branches
and pools of ruffled water and where
a jay would exchange its shock of blue
with heaven and gaunt plumes of milk-
weed would fly apart and scatter in
search of lift like aimless strands of cloud.

Foretoken

The sun's dragging the last
of its light like a tattered shawl
across the sky, brushing aside
day's tired air that's nestled
in the spaces that sit between
the understory's branches and
I can see how each leaf, for a
moment, is finely gilded, tail-
spun and lifted, displaying a
gift of color better suited to
a downfallen moon or a garden
lantern softly illuminated by
candle-light, at least until the
time of their fall and sweet
convulsion, as they settle back,
pieta-still, into a fallacy of green
and then wondering, in their bright
stillness, just how much closer
we might be until the hour of their
decadent descent and breathless ruin.

Autumnal

Sunlight intrudes quietly, slipping past
the morning fog that hangs motionless,
like a latticework of bridal-veil white,
extending in silence across the shaved
lawns and clouding over the blood-orange
blemish of chrysanthemums and porches
girdled in vibrant strands of bittersweet.
Now, all things appear as imprecise as
memory, drifting between sleeps, like
the whimsical sail of a solitary flicker,
trellises laden with the heads of flowers
still heavy with leaf and blossom, or the
lopsided scarecrows attired in flannel
and brittle stalks of corn, feigning motion,
leaning on lightless lampposts as if they're
enduring some inconsolable loss and
grieving for what once was, or perhaps
they're listening to a sad tune whistled from
afar, before they gather the thick assembly
of leaves, lacquered by fog, and scatter
them in the far reaches of the fields
where, exiled and bereft of hope, they
can settle in silence, like the remains of
this day, and slowly marry with the soil.

After Listening to Copland's *Appalachian Spring*

Lost in afterthought, I paused
for a time in the linen light,
and listened to the cadence
of the landscape and the low
thrum of the turning earth
as an afternoon of high clouds
descended and unlatched
evening's door, revealing
the last of its wind-combed
grasses—each blade broken
and bending towards earth—
the purpling splotches of
elderberry, tangled bowers
of bittersweet and the first-
blood velvet of sumacs; the
jubilant yellow of birches
and maples, eerily underlit
and waiting to fall away;
and the early autumn air,
still redolent with the
profuse, deep-rooted
scents of stubble and soft
rain, and certain that a day
such as this, when the ordinary
seems to undress itself into
something exquisite and
hauntingly beautiful, is not
so distant from the divine.

Bloodgood Maple

How their branches seem
to extend without burden
in the lengthening light,
their star-shaped leaves
of deepest burgundy,
weightless, more form
than texture, surrendering
to autumn air in such a way
that it's difficult to discern
where leaf-tip ends and
shade begins; until, wind-
jostled, they flutter like
wisps of cordovan dust
out into a blue expanse
of emptiness—traversing
the chasm between having
been and soon becoming—
showing us a way forward,
letting go without regret
or anguish, and knowing
this world will be made
whole again from those
very things that have
been taken or freely given.

Latitudes

Here, the morning sky appears
like a mosaic of coral-colored glass
assembled by the fonds of sabal
palms, then lightly polished and
pressed into a thin-set of Biscayne
blue. Low clouds stretch in after-
glow across the horizon as if they
were lit from within and everywhere
there's a gross profusion of broad-
petaled blossoms and tangled shoals
of under-leaf, enveloping a world
still coveting summer and overrun
with scents of fresh citrus, clove
and a pleasurable alchemy of salt
mingled with the damp tang of ash.
Stranded here, I'd gladly risk losing
this artifice of malarial light, and
embrace a world and weather in free-
fall, many miles distant and weighted
with darkness, where bare boughs
stand cloaked in shadow and you can
lose yourself in sweater-cold air
that is grizzled with frost and woven
like cornsilk into the very fabric
of things, and all light is forever
fading and serves to illuminate only
what has been lost or remains absent.

Odyssey

On such days as this there's
a deeper sense of something
arriving and leaving as the
slow sweep of wind unveils
the bruised beauty of every
leaf transforming them from
a canopy of weathered green
into a dreamscape of russet-
orange and star-burst yellow,
and though each burns brightly
and, for all my years upon
this earth, still arrests the eye
and haunts the heart, I know
the fate of such divine splendor,
harboring a deciduous darkness
that masses between their
contorted branches and braided
roots where autumn light falters
and tendrils of frost glaze the
leaf scatter that's soon lifted
and dispersed like tiny skiffs
that delicately spiral, crest
then diminish with distance
before gliding into a fallen
world of wind-spun ruin.

Cue the Barbizon

With night drawing on, I settle
in silence to gather my half-
formed thoughts of an afternoon's
fleeting apparitions, where the sky
more resembled a reflecting pool
of standing water than a chamber
of frosted air and how the would-
be artist inside of me retraced the
very way day, in its rustic autumn
palette, slowly turned inward upon
itself as if in mourning, and, standing
apart in distant splendor, an outpost
of woodland birches and the straw-
gold bounty of sugar maples drinking
in the last of the impoverished light,
all tethered to muddy fields and the
dried stalks of distant rushes, fluttering
and loosely feathered, or, closer in,
an unkempt garden overflowing
with the fragrant froth of asters
freckled with enough bees to
replace the nearer stars all while
a downpour of dusk, donning a
grackle's plumage, descended,
and how each image emerged
with the type of grandeur that
held the heart and offered both
hope and promise in a world that
provides so very little of either.

All In (on) Autumn

Even twilight seems to hesitate
and look over its shoulder wistfully
at the remains of this day before
the sun slips below the edge
of evening in a blaze so brilliant
that the emerging stars appear
to be little more than embers
predictably rising, but even you,
who believes that, unlike the
elusive, soft-timbred air of early
summer, this is surely the saddest
of seasons where everything is
long-settled, tethered and held
close to ground, including the
orchard's trees, lumbering down-
hill with their gnarled branches
laden with spoiled fruit, and wisps
of fog hovering just above fields
of frost where a few dark birds
have descended like flecks of ash
upon the ground, and how, after
all, it is doing little more than
turning from the sun and courting
an uneasy emptiness, determined
to unhear a dying earth's songs
of rapture that eventually, in
diminishing light, will come to
settle and roost deep inside the heart.

A Winter Offering

A transient wind falters
in its leave taking and
return from a winter sky,
arcing above a low sun
and a world of diminished
light to whittle away at
the nearer edge of heaven,
exposing a reservoir of
unruffled air brighter
than even mid-summer
might provide, fore-
shadowing something
other than an unborn season
of want and longing; then,
stumbling blindly through
frost-bitten air, comes back
in rudderless jubilation,
tripping across the silvering
hills and fields of trampled
grass, and slows to a
shamble as it empties the
all of it into these still
waters where its deliberate
pour slowly stirs the last
of autumn's easy gold,
scoring the surface with
blossoms of harlequin
yellow, before the sweet
vanishings of the broad
tongues and rudderless
stems down-drifting back
into their dark, fertile beds
where no light lives.

Replenishment

Caught in the cold holler
between seasons, I'm greeted
by a week's worth of forty-
degree days and the morning
air's just cold enough to
discourage dawdling, pushing
me past the eerie stillness of
the marsh, a desolate shoreline
and the soft drawl of tides towards
a horizon that's starless, full-
ominous, and a few breaths
shy of splendor, when dawn's
pale, preemptive light labors
for lift from beyond the tree-
line like a fledgling rising
furtively from its nest before—
there it is—the all-in ascent
westwards with wings extended
in a burst of incendiary scatter
brushing past the ruffled edges
of some cast-away clouds and
giving way to what's left of
a waning moon and an evening
sky while I stand and bow in
dumb rapture before it with
a tired, shrunken heart that
had given in to the weight
of the world and fallen, with-
out appeal, to a place that
was near empty and something
so much less than whole.

The Connecticut in Winter

It is Hartford seen in purple light.
—Wallace Stevens

Silence tested by the soft applause
of birds, the long, tidal river meanders
unhurried, carving a fault line between
a wound of ocean and a distant finger-
tip of lake. Moats a parish of six, corner-
cupboard states, gliding past what little
is left of soft-shouldered hills and hollows,
farmland and short-cropped fields and
a landscape forever lost to trespass.
Here, near its final leg, comes a reprieve
of level land as it courses through the
ox-bows and spill-ways drunk with
dusk, glides past the windows of despondent
buildings and concrete trusses straddling
a river that's surely wondering what's
now left of nature before it's ambushed
by salt, fatigued fingers fumbling to
hold on to these quivering images
and wanting nothing more than to
finally release them into swirling
eddies and shallow pools of purple light.

January Thaw

Weeks into the first month of
the year and winter's just departed
for holiday, leaving to us a flawless
basin of blue buttressed by dense
boughs and a changeable breeze that's—
how best to describe it?—medicinal,
warming ice-hardened furrows
and rutted roads and itching to
transform the terraced hills into
a tracery of green that's just this
side of hay-loft yellow when the
afternoon air offers up the milled
fragrance of freshly cut cedar and
the sudden refrain of bird-song
that trips down the air, not unlike
the way that we, against all reason,
come to hope that an obstinate grief
will somehow ease and leave our
hearts, in some strange way, refreshed,
even near-grateful, with a discernible
diminishing of hurt and the fear of a
life-long pain without reprieve or purpose.

Passiontide

Nothing could have prepared me for a day such as
this and the many forms that wonder takes, where
the fringe of woodland skirts the festive brew of
colors, emerging scents and languid currents of the
tidal flats and where the wide-crowned trees, with
their collars of moss, still stand large and leafless,
swaying like tines raking clouds in faint rustle across
a sky of unbridled blue, and allowing sunlight to
spill over and in-between the branches while a
warm wind treads past the gnarled limbs of cedars
balancing thin baskets of ice before heading across
the farther fields of tall grass to lift laundry, ruffle
tidal pools and gather up the scattered plunder
that's freely offered by a newly softened earth.

Restoration

Wanting for warmth, evening's
wonderstruck and has folded in
upon itself and, in the darkness,
snow's falling in deafening silence,
flake upon flake upon frenetic flake
laundering the air with a will
to soften the earth's hard edges
and bring abundance and beauty
back into this world, obliterating
bleakness, ghosting the landscape,
rounding out the wide wounds
that wish to hold it, while windless
hands, in hushed assembly, rebuild
stacks of firewood, raise snow-
capped roofs, level tilted porches
and add heft to doorsteps bordered
by evergreens and the thin, top-
most branches of leafless shrubs
and in the farther field a few
boulders remain exposed just
above the bluing drifts like heifers
foraging for thin winter grasses
when a stream of light from
somewhere beyond my line
of sight leaks through the darkness
slowly revealing the world's
second, better self just returned
from the afterlife, stark and still
and miraculously luminous.

Something More Than Winter
(Weighs Upon Me)

Slowed by missteps and an unshakeable
grief, I'm approaching the trail's end,
watching the waning light dust the
top of the tree line where a few solitary
leaves of Klimt gold flutter like torches
set upon the crowns of beech, while
a congregation of juncos, shaped like
sable flames, seem to blur and bend
the low-hanging branches, noting how
even the wind's weighted, too, with
frost and wood-smoke and rank
with leaf decay. In the further field,
snow, as soft as fly ash, is swept across
the thin shell of ice that lacquers the
pond, adhering to the edges of tomb-
stones leaning away from wind and
much too close to earth, and I pause
to consider how all seems to be near
or at an ending and so takes on the
season's muted hues of heart-sore grey,
and I see what little light is left to this
day, knowing, too, that I've done few
things well in this life and that it
is not so easy to displace loss, or
to cast aside regrets or to somehow
ease the even greater weight of
those I still carry deep inside me.

Transformation

It is a solitary watch the crow keeps
and with an appraiser's eye surveys
the changing contour of the earth,
the blond brook that fitfully sleeps
beneath the ice; the undaunted way
snow falls—a month's worth
within a day.

The silence seems to coax the cold
and draws down the darker firmament
towards a stock-still earth;
the oak, whose upper branches hold
a curious ornament,
has lessened in height, grown in girth;
the different ways

this storm reconfigures all we knew
into the strange and less familiar.
Orchards turned to stubble; earth-
bowed junipers are ice-jeweled
fountains of colored glass and, there,
pressed to window, wind's attached
a chrome-encrusted, blue-green spray.

Scarcity

Winter's laying claim to earth and
leaving a trail of snow-dust upon
the hills, and it seems all things
have become more familiar with
grief and going and are now being
hitched to the hereafter by an
unfaltering cold that's hardening
sodden furrows into mounds of
velour glistening in transient
light, while the sad soliloquy of
a grosbeak, perched upon the felled
branches of an evergreen, probes
the depth of this day's emptiness
and I find myself suddenly abandoned,
too, and wondering if I have ever
possessed enough faith in myself
or in this world, then continuing
down a narrow path towards
the edge of the tree-line and the
swale of valley that dips beyond,
making note of the vivid brush-
strokes of my breath, and how each
grows shorter than the one before.

Winter Night in New England

The air, that night, felt
as if the world itself had
paused to take in a sky that
was the perfect mix of clouds
and starlight and all movement
seemed transfixed except
for the loose calligraphy
of our breath lifting into
vapor and dissolving within
the opulent halos of the
lampposts. And then
watching the broken body
of darkness in that tender
hour, full-drunk, swallow
dusk's last vial of violet,
stumble down the alleyways
between brick buildings
and the brighter pour of
Flemish blue and brass
from lower shop windows
moments before we were
overtaken by the sudden
applause of snow falling
in synchronized spirals with
flakes, I swear, the size of
sparrows that you cupped
into your gloved hands,
wanting to hold onto that
evening's miracle before
it perished and all drifted
back into the silent embrace
of an indeterminate wind.

II. The Sea and Sky

Here I am again with my old friend, the sea;
it is always endless and beautiful.
It is really the thing in Nature which restores . . .

—Claude Debussy

A Bountiful Silence

I love being silent as much as I love being in the silence.
—David Carroll

It is the in-between hour when
daylight slowly turns to lose
itself in the embrace of evening,
and I've come in search of the
stillness that lingers between
the swell and hushed exodus
of the tides; those rare, fugitive
moments soon after discourse
is diffused and beaches itself
and time grows slack and one
must work harder to hear the
breath of an elusive earth exhaling
in the rasp of brittle, ice-crusted
reeds, the amplified rocking
of the wind in search of freight,
and the faint wails of white-
winged gulls, then gazing back
at the illuminated squares of
cottage windows where short-
sighted day has hurried to warm
itself, nodding drowsily by fire-
light, having left such endearments
to those of us who willingly
welcome the gradual lilt of loss,
the betrayal of hope and the
louder expanse of silence.

The Evanescent

How best to preserve a day that's unfurling
in lateral light, spreading across the water
like sterling poured from a crucible fastened
to the horizon and the frantic flares that
madly scatter and assault the eye or the
graceful egret, with its wide, sensual wings,
appraising with indifference the coastline's
stillness and the open spaces that seem to
float between inlets and the thick bouquets
of violet impasto—glazed clusters of mussels
exposed by the receding tide—all bound together
by translucent strands of sugar kelp and the
sweeter scents of conifers and cedar and the
sound of winter reeds softly clattering in a
brittle wind while I stand awestruck and
thankful that this luminous and enduring world
still has the power to stir the soul, now convinced
this life is one worth living even though such
marvel and wonder are difficult to keep and
appear to be continually moving away from us?

Moon Bound

Day gave way to the tender blessing of an October night,
with warm gusts lifting me atop the moon's ghostly white
saddle, and we rose past rings of fog and cosmic dust
into the unknowable air, a thing both strange and miraculous,

and the day's many burdens lifted with pleasurable ease
as I cleared the urban wild, the crowns of leafless trees,
crossed frosted meadow-grass and sea-swells glazed with light
the holy hush found in vagrant clouds and the brighter

assemblies of teeming stars—steadfast and luminous—
while the threaded transit of a stray comet's exodus
from heaven led me to consider the narrowing of night
and our sad, solitary journeys in sun-seeming flight,

each departing this mirthless world, like dream-mighty Icarus,
with his down-drawn wings of wax in day's brazen light.

Reconciliation

Barely any sounds or light in the sky
just yet and there's an uncommon
stillness as if the dull, dark whole
of the world has taken an indrawn
breath while a crescent moon, stalled
in its slow transit, spills its feeble
light across the brooding hills and
the water and I'm wondering why
it is that I sometimes feel better suited
to the world at an hour such as this
when silence takes hold, and, knowing
how memories become more elusive
as we age, I am somehow able to
more clearly recall those times I lost
what mattered most in this life while
watching days shamble into months
and months into years and you tell
yourself that all that goes missing
happens for a reason and that there's
a valiant purpose to be found in grief
and anguish until that moment of
quiet retreat gives way to a bird
yearning haplessly to lift itself from
the surface of the water, the rhythmic
knocking of a loosely tethered boat,
the muffled unfurling of a flag
wakened by wind, and the louder
foment of the mid-summer tide
rising and rushing towards shore
and the brazen detritus of the living,
lifting and cleansing the heart
before it slowly settles back to body.

Fortuity

Now, just as the world
wears out and night leaks
into day, shadows sliding
in silent trespass across a
desolate landscape and a
lethargic wind—day's final
wingbeat—settles under
the eaves, hold close those
bright astonishments that
still beguile and bewilder
and are sprinkled like rare
tokens of hope throughout
the world. Draw a certain
comfort from those exquisite
endearments and illusory fragments
of dream-stuff that help to
make our rush to ruin bearable;
and then, for all that, tell me
again, beneath the haze of
woodsmoke and smudge of
star light, how life will once
again come to greenness and
what form forgiveness takes.

Sea Drift

Something of this place stays with me still
and the worn haversack of memory is unable
to carry it away. It's pinned beneath a world
that's beyond forgetting and smelling always
of salted brume and rusted metal and the
nearly sweet scent of diesel fuel and oil that
would lazily drift upon the surface of the
water in mylar plumes of Prussian blue, iris
and ornate bronze like eerie, non-ephemeral
rainbows spooling and dismembering beneath
the splintered shadows of the docks or along
the scavenged banks that housed the worn
implements of nautical toil: ragged tents of
canvas, cables, traps, anchors and mangled
tackle; and standing further on, the brighter
scatter of bundled sails, tall as cypress trees,
casting tapered shadows that seemed to slip
across muscled wakes and the crest of waves
while gulls would wheel and curl above us
in garbled greetings, their manic staccato
silenced by the approaching thrum and brute
rumble of trawlers with limbs outstretched
like a trapeze artist seeking balance, and,
on wind-still days, crooked sheds releasing
their musty odors of decay, and disfigured
cottages, bereft of shingles, adorned with
flaking, chalk-white shutters and rooflines
powdered with grains of mica in midday
light and piers punched deep into the glazed
lather of rockweed and slime where earth's
rich effulgence had been preserved and
was slowly disgorged while faint clouds of
sulfur would silently rise and fill our lungs.

La Voglia di Sognare
(The Desire to Dream)

Tonight, beneath a quiet moon,
I listen to the small boats rock
themselves to sleep upon moss-
green waters; the dull, muffled
plunk of wood feeling for wood
followed by a prolonged silence
as a breeze rises from the rushes.
This night they float lightly in a
world without compass, no longer
weighted by stout oars or the
sorrows they have helped to ferry
from land to sea and back again
and, in imprecise undulation,
with wide mouths agape, they
now freely dream of returning
from distant lands, with heavy
hulls sunk in sand, laden with
spoils as bright as Venus in a
winter sky. And so, at this idle
hour, when all things are nearest
to emptiness, unburdened by grief
or grievances, I ask for nothing
more than the chance to hold on to
this moment before all dissolves or
drifts away into day's bright oblivion.

Home Bound

A house, with a light fog laid against it, sits
near-hidden except for the dormer windows
that appear to be adrift in early morning air—
more ruffled oculus than precise square—
with their amber light rising and dipping
in the darkness, floating eerily above
the bleached bodies of overturned boats and
piles of weathered timber and in that moment
I'm holding hope like day's first light close
to my chest, recalling the want for wonder
that led me away from land to where the
waves always seem to retract in a slow
sprawl of silence and recalling the day before
when I was struck by the ornate contrails
of cloud descending like pilasters against
a flawless canopy of balsam-blue sky and
the land fell away before I found myself held
by the pull of the marsh mud, forcing me to pause
and look more closely at those things nearest
to earth and the carnage left behind by the
outgoing tide, and each slow, ponderous step
revealed how all that is taken from this
world is eventually given back and replenished
along with the smaller glories scattered about
us like the slender sorcerer's silhouette standing
motionless in the fog-bright air, its steadfast gaze
focused upon the viscid oil that spreads across
the surface of the tidal flats where light and
dark mingle in water that, some time ago, had
crested and reached a level it could only forsake
before the bird turned skywards to pray for
a day of plenty with no intention of moving on.

Consequential Light

Undone by days such as this—
still-becoming—I can see how
dawn does not break so much
as it pauses to consider its
tepid trespass before striking
the heart with its long arc
of light and then easing itself
up and over the ridgeline
like a luminous quilt, softly
unfolding and settling back
down across the contours
of the earth and soon after,
sensing there's a need for still
more beauty in this world,
rearranges the clouds like large,
terra cotta pots that it fills
with the drowsy heads of tiered,
mid-summer blossoms before
placing them upon the lateral
sill of the horizon moments
before a soft applause of blue
breaks out and darkness, startled
and maimed and still thirsting
for dream, retracts and seeks a
makeshift peace in morning shadow.

A Nameless Loss

Falling one after the other
like spent embers from the upper
air, a conclave of crows return
from their distant nests, recounting
someone's misfortune that they're
unable to fix. I'm watching their
macabre dance with wings lifting
their downfallen figures in and out
of shade as if they were seeking to
somehow rise up and leave their
bodies altogether before they suddenly
glide back towards the open space
near a shoreline of drab green water
and gather in a motionless stupor,
forming a dark circle where they
bend to stillness and, with unmended
hearts, they call down others in
a graceless gesture to replace them
as they look away and fly off
like discarded dreams, having
mourned as best they could, without
any promise of help or healing.

Fog

Seeking a place to pause,
fog wheels and eludes the
white tongues of tides,
bedding down the tiny
boats and cottages into
graphite-colored graves.
Sky descending or water
rising and an abstract earth's
releveling. Sight defers
to the muffled drone and
brutish pace of a small boat's
motor and the delicate wake
that curls into ear. Even
the further field's pink blaze
of fireweed runs to gauze in
oyster-gleam. The waning
of form to specter draws
us into this aberration of
tidal calm, glistening in
ornate light like some
exquisite vestment woven
from ever-lasting dew,
viscid pearl and wheat-
yellow strands of spider silk.

After the Fall
(A Bruise Remains)

Watching the calamity of colors at dusk
converge then hastily expand as if the
universe has gone garish and finally
ruptured and dumbly divided itself,
while cloudbursts of plum pilfer the
green from the crowns of trees and
flooded fields and then steadily rise
in an ominous cloud of madras to
obliterate the last oasis of blue,
continuing to unfurl like a spiraling
trail of smoke from the spent head
of a match-stick. Ailing and love-
sick, I'm left to wondering if this day's
dwindling and demise, like my heart,
will ever heal before evening over-
spreads a pained sky like oil oozing
from the bottom of a rusted barrel,
knowing sometimes the world, despite
our best efforts, will only bequeath to us
blemishes and bruises and something
that's so much closer to loss than healing.

Dissolution

Weather-worn and woven
from threads of hay and
meadow grass, the bedraggled
nest had once been bound
by dollops of mud and a
lattice-work of lichen. And
yet, here it lies, death's
trinket, tucked and tousled
beneath a bed of bleeding
hearts like a hollow urn,
broken and unfixable and
inching towards sediment,
having once housed, behind
the soft lift and fall of leaves,
songs that perhaps washed
like rain water into the hearts
of those who, near nightfall,
were fortunate enough to
take in the last light lingering
and savor the palpable grace
before it, too, slipped back
into garden like a slowly
departing grief that is harder
to forget than to remember.

Beholden

There can be but one teacher—nature.
She must always be consulted.
                —Camille Pissarro

I'm wondering how best to preserve
this day when I find myself summoned
outside into the warming light, tossing
my net beyond the low islands and
the jagged edge of the Sound,
hoping its threads return in gilded
attire, yielding a tangle of blessings
culled from both sea and hollow
that are a mix of old-growth splendor
and the commonplace, while I fall
back to silence, watching the way
the morning light breaks apart and
is then quickly redrawn by wind gusts
that blur and wrinkle the surface of
the water, and entranced by the soft
rustling of the beach grass and
the tang of salt-scented air while
white-capped tides are suffused with
the same mussel-blue hue as the
open fist of sky and seeing how
both air and water are stitched together
by these clamorous gulls rising in
rapture then swooning towards shore
and asking what more can be done
other than to try and somehow slow
earth's hurry and call summer back.

Reassessment

Unperturbed by the tidal surge
and coastal gales, a tern glides
past with a fluid grace I can only
envy when suddenly it rises
and arcs backwards against
the wind as if it was telling
itself to return and set aside
its daytime tasks and to look
more closely at the Gorgon
wreaths of bladderwrack,
cauldrons of tidal foam and
soft-spooling eddies of nickel-
blue waters, and reconsider
the silent plenty of light that's
been spliced from the waves
and then applied like glaze upon
the peninsula's coarse under-
belly of granite, festooned with
periwinkles, snails and purple
colonies of mussels, and even
the near-distant beds of sea
roses that are clipped by wind
and curve in a florid crescent
away from the harbor, realizing
this stretch of shoreline merits
more than a four-square fly-by
and nautical salutations composed
of strident sharps and flats.

Consecration

Morning's hoarded a season's worth
of opulence and now gathers the last
of its new-found gold—a nomadic
moon yolked by a bridle of fog to
the far horizon—and a resolute blue
toils in its rise upon dusty wings of
rose-pink mostly, like the beveled
lip of a conch, muted colors coating
the slope of snow-covered hills and
infusing tongues of ice suspended
from the eaves, glazing the bare boughs
that have yet to dress themselves in
a frantic blush of green and cadmium
yellow, highlighting the vivid flame
of paper birch that expired last night
in a frantic wind that's now hushed
in its passing, soft as prayer, out upon
the harbor's still waters while the
world holds its breath and dark
birds keep to their silent vigil and
seem to ask that we, too, wade out
with grace into the light, praising
the world before us and holding
close divine days such as this when,
call it what you will, the earth exults
and all is reclaimed by heaven.

Castaway

Arrived here without compass,
having tumbled, pilotless, along
the seabed beneath the rusted
freighter's long sweep of nets
and the knocking of the tides
and suddenly finds itself, with
morning nearly gone, a puzzle
to solve by a grey gull webbing
its way from water. I run my
fingers across its abandoned
body—thinking it could be a
narwhal's tiny tusk, some
ornate chalice or small-sword
from the rococo—and note its
assemblage of whorled striations,
spears and spire, crafted in
elegant torque and defying
practical geometry with its
fillet design and wide, glossy
wing—doused in a shade of
pink more exquisite than any
summer sunrise we might
care to imagine—curling into
a fluted grotto where neither
light nor color linger and
where the maker often
withdrew to weather this
blundering world though
there's more than an ending
here, as I pause to listen to
the sea's haunting breath

and its song of an aging
grief, heart-forgotten, that's
emptied out of it and
still wanting to be heard.

Bermuda Nocturne

The causeway's awash in changeable light;
tide's barely audible, sea-foam white.
Air's pearl-strung with tears of salt and husks
of aromatic hibiscus. Low lying clouds extend dusk
like an oil cloth across the western

horizon, heaven's colors slowly lessening
and I can sense something
more than the coming on of night
and an abounding silence, while
ominous sea birds rise eerily from nests.

Wind's falling away and does little to suppress
the absolute and ungodly emptiness
that lingers inside me. A halo of dust-dancing light
from an unhooded moon rises to a height
where stars slowly dim and are then extinguished.

Al Fin del Dia

Clouds hover like a second, higher
horizon above a dead-calm harbor
where the curved bows of wooden
boats imperceptibly rise and fall
as if they're in a soundless sleep
and night pushes on, gradually
overtaking the inlet's claret luster
moments before the last of summer's
thin light is reeled in and, barely
audible above a listless wind,
the feeble ping of rigging cuffing
masts and transforming this
moment into one of becalmed
marvel when all burdens appear
to be lifted just the way the misfit
moon was later released from
the sprawl of marsh holding more
than its fair share of luster scoring
the surface of the water while a
fevered spill of swallows rose
to savor the last light lingering
and the deepening peace of dusk.

Flood Plain

Coaxed by the garish sheen
of Versailles gold that's coating
the near horizon, I take the day's
final hour out walking with no
assurance of return. I'm falling
east heading towards that healing
space where sea and salt marsh
marry and a path of ridged shells
rises from water to where wind
combs the leaves of wind-spun
trees with branches entwined,
some leaning sideways as if they
are preparing to resurrect a moon
that remains hidden from view or
perhaps they, too, are eager to bury
a season's worth of burdens in a
damp coffer of silt, continuing on
with this broken life as silently as
the channels that run past shuttered
cottages leading into reed pools
where, weighted with salt, they
leisurely spool for a time, like
pebble-struck rings, and then
feign rest, provoking an uneasy
pause where one can still sense
the slow leaking of sound and
the absence of so much more
than light while now-distant
tides fall away in a tremulous
thinning like a grief that's been
graciously erased only to return
with little care for what comes after.

Earthly Blue Sublime

Delighting in dalliance
and the grand malaise
of mid-summer mornings,
she abandons her bed
and rises from slumber
in bright stillness and then,
with head set upon her shoulder,
gazes out her window before
donning vestments, rearranging
a vase of larkspur and, in a
drowsy flourish, eases night's
hold over heaven by extinguishing
the stars and tiny torches of
lamplight, even as she opals
dew and leaves parts of herself
tucked within the pockets of
the tides and inside the colder
currents of woodland waters,
then expands ever more luminous
towards the far horizon engulfed
by the sun's yellow ravishing,
color floating up and out of her
body, birthing worlds of sea-glass
green; other times, closer in,
she'll extend her slim fingers to
purposefully warm the kettle's
metal belly with petals of blue-
orange flame, glaze the house's
closed windows and soften the
hard edges of the here and now.

Backwash

The shoreline is littered with motifs
from the Art Nouveau, assembled
from an elaborate tangle of cattails
and matted grasses whiplashed and
set upon the sand in sinuous scatter,
forming intricate arches and arabesques
festooned with shells, fishbones
and the nautical embellishments
of tangled nets held together by
crusted medallions of tackle—all
gilded by a mid-day sun. And, as
so often happens, I find myself
once again attempting to interpret
the language of the sea and stitch
together pieces of a world that
remains bruised and broken
and in desperate need of repair,
as loss continues to assert itself
before giving way to receding
tides and a deep, perishable stillness,
when I can better sense its stealthy
advance from the putrid breath
of marsh towards the water's edge
where light dissolves back into
light before reappearing as wind-
borne fleece upon this spit of land.

How Darkness Fell

In June 2023, large swaths of the United States were covered by wind-blown smoke from wildfires burning throughout Canada.

It's as if a vast expanse of dusk
had assailed the world and
morning's brief beauty had
convulsed and been emptied
of light, leaving behind a
coarsened landscape of dead-
water gray and bird-less air
that carried the pungent odor
of smoldering ash, while, in
the distance, the vague outlines
of buildings appeared like
headstones that loomed over
a haze of blight, and above it all,
suspended in eerie isolation,
a ruined sun that drifted in
and out of a sky choked with
ruffled cloud like some unalloyed
coin that had been minted to
commemorate hell's handiwork
at a time when it's hard not to
think that something more than
day is dissolving, silent as an
eclipse, into vulgar darkness.

The Quelling

I've often longed for an evening
such as this when moonlight gilds
the pathway with a bronze varnish
that washes past the woodshed
and floods into pasture before
pooling beneath a dry-stone wall
where a few leafless trees seem
to arc towards a lovelorn earth
and I hold certain, in the damp
stillness that follows dusk, that
this night, even with its raw silence,
will never know loneliness or lack
for wonder with its delirious ballet
of bats, a wood-pecker's rapid-fire
ambush of a bark-less tree, the divine
presence of slowly emerging stars
and the purr of wind pulling down
cooler air that tastes like ash upon
the tongue and will be taken in and
later, deep in sleep, enter the blood.

With Apologies from the Atlantic

Tonight I imagine you, a continent
distant, weathering a world on
another coast while welcoming
with grace the muted purl of the
Pacific, loose strands of hair blown
back from your head like garlands
of Spanish moss, hands outstretched
and holding the last of the hurt that
had washed up with me years before
and that I left with you to mend and
heal and how well I remember your
stating how the tides often bring to
us chance blessings and how each
of us has a right to even a few
moments of happiness though,
I had reminded you, the tides can
be fickle things, too, and sometimes
depart with no intention of returning,
and now, beneath a pining moon,
I take in the receding jade waters
and maritime reek of the alien
Atlantic, watching light leaving
then returning, and wondering why
it has taken me until now to ask
for your forgiveness knowing full
well it would be good to love again
if only I could find my way back.

Steps from Water

The sea floor's exposed
in saline glitter and clouds of foam,
and the air is thick with the fetid breath
of marsh and death's
ensconced in tidal pools of broken shell and bone
while the shoreline's transposed

by gnarled clusters of olive-green
bladderwrack. Their pungent
reek and the odor of the marsh
meet mid-air, along with a rash
of flies, tiny accents
in mackerel-blue sheen.

Now, no longer a harbor
but what comes after—
a glistening expanse of opal grain,
sand spits and barnacles that remain
stranded above water;
pursed mouths of waves crusted over.

Moonlight unevenly scours
the overturned hulls of boats and the bay's
a paten of pale gold and black;
wind eels its way thru marsh and back,
the rank smells of decay—
what water now moves towards.

Giving Way

Wind's abated and gone bird-dog
still while curtains shudder back
to stillness and even a gunslinger
sparrow has abandoned its song
as if certain passages were in need
of revision while the morning tides,
reduced to murmur, slink away in
slow retreat, taking hurt and hurry
with them, and I'm wondering
what else heaven might offer
when bands of sunlight ease past
the clouds like plaster oozing
from behind long strips of lath
only to dissolve in a harlequin
display across the tidal flats
as leaves of fevered red and
fire-light yellow drift down
and settle among the coastal
grasses or cling like wilted
blossoms to the barbed stems
of shoreline roses and I stand,
with fewer days before me,
dumbfounded by the right-
well flare and splendor of this
hour even as autumn lessens,
though I cannot fathom why
time and a nearly healed soul—
one weightless and the other
weighing only a few grams—
should prod me from behind
and urge me to press on.

Capitulation

Shoreline is shrinking and the
shuttered cottages are ghosted
by mists drifting upward from
channels of mud-softened
marsh like tawdry shrouds
that appear more pallid smudge
than luminous pearl and the frayed
tassels of common reeds, that
once rustled high in pale blue
air, are now arched in supplication
like martyrs leaning closer to
an imperfect earth as all the
world's submerged in a kind of
deadfall between seasons without
the gift of sound or movement,
minding the air's prolonged
undulations and the deepening
stillness of the water, until the
sudden sprawl of a heron laboring
to lift its bright weight in stony
silence and, once air borne,
watching its avian form shape-
shift back into the abandoned
light of the back-water and I
find myself somewhere between
awe and surrender, asking for
that moment back, yet knowing
it, too, like a life, will be
erased and given up to ether.

In Low Light

The tides have fallen back from shore
and the harbor's become a sprawl of
whimsical ruin, wide and still and without
ruffle, and I can see how its slender
shine stretches out and traverses the
Sound on its way past dry-docked
trawlers towards the horizon where
it bends then fractures at some unseen
angle towards a heaven that's draped
in coastal-fog grey and the space
between air and water is difficult to
discern since these are more pallid,
impoverished clouds than Constable's
bloated spires of celestial splendor
and you fear the beatific blue that once
emerged between them may soon be
extinguished altogether because this
is, after all, a soft-fallen, yet cold and
comfortless, winter in New England
where light is always receding and
afternoon air is wet and weighted
and without song, as the few remaining
birds are all mortuary black and muted
bluster and beauty must be something
wished for, pillaged or cobbled together
from the tideline's thatched decay.

Windward

Day's drifting away from its mooring,
sails bloated by a gentle gust pushing
it from behind, leaving in its wake
the shoreline's spectacle of ghostly
shells, marine metals and the lunar
stillness of the harbor as it pursues
the channel's aquatic light where a
nomadic wind lifts the waves up
and out of themselves promising
easeful passage into the brightening
air where they can, perhaps, see more
closely how an early morning sky
arcs away from—then bends back
towards—itself and the terrible quiet
of distant swells, glistening like
fresh bundles of hay spread across
a rutted field, while solicitous gulls
hover and wheel above me, assessing
the precise distance of the tide's
tinsel flare from shore and I stand
motionless as thoughts slow, and
I immerse myself in the sudden
upswell of scents weighted with
salt, tomorrow's rain and the sweet
decay dislodged from somewhere
beyond the periphery of the marsh,
slowly retreating then curling back
to remind me how the world can
strike the heart then just as quickly
fall away while time moves on
without us and how this day's
exquisite undoing will, piece
by piece, fall to memory but
will never be ours to live again.

Dispersal

—based on artwork by Eoin Lane

It's difficult to recall a day such as this when
a sky of breathtaking blue has gone gossamer,
steadily dwindling and giving way to clouds

that seem to dissolve in an expansive sleep
of water, leaving to me this fugitive landscape and
the brief quieting that comes when day offers up

the last of its splendor and, for a moment, heaven
becomes a place that's indistinguishable from
the contour of the earth and the sudden spill of the

divine presses against all things, as the tide softly
swells then retracts, haunting the soul with its diffused
murmur, and a warm wind, hushed and heavy-hearted,

too, in its passing, extinguishes the last light before giving
way to a lone sentinel's eerie bellow, leaving the weighted air
infused with plum-rose splatter and the pungent smell of pine.

Annalist

From a deserted shoreline,
I watch a moonless sky darken
and regift to the ocean a tapestry
of wind-battered blue embroidered
with a tracery of gold as waves press
then unroll it in frenetic shimmer,
wanting to sustain day's last light
and early evening calm and, some-
times, at moments such as this, I
become exiled from myself, the
tyranny of this one life and serve
as the vessel that holds the hour's
transitory splendor, making note
of the weight of salted air and
the pungent fragrance rising
from tangled hedges of privet,
the hurtle and melodic falter of
the tides, and the delirious spirals
of swallows at dusk, growing
smaller with distance, wanting
to help each of them find their
way into memory and word.

Coastal Fog

It seemed to pause before gathering itself
and then moving on and consuming a sky
of fathomless blue as we sought to puzzle
out some semblance of a horizon or even
a patch of ruined light, enthralled by its
delicate destruction and otherworldly
darkness as if it were God's do-over breaking
across the edge of ocean and erasing the
waves that moments before were hurdling
the jetty, then erasing the shoreline, cottages
and even the lavish plumes of hydrangea
as its opaque mass slowly passed over us
and continued on in search of refuge some-
where near the muddled beauty of the marsh
and the inlet's aimless channels of still water,
leaving only the faint, aromatic drift of rose-
scented air, the murmuring spill and milk-
white flare of waves coming to help mend
and heal what was left of the world with gauze
woven from spindrift, splinters of sand and
delicate threads of tidal grass and gold dust.

Reclamation

Hard to imagine that the day would end like this—
the way the morning began with thunderheads
rising in silence from a narrowing fissure of sky,
extinguishing the ascending light, and then advancing
in dark velocity across the Sound, exhorting agitated
waves to advance, pummel and vanquish the shore,
scavenging and reshaping inlets that shackle marsh
and then unleash its dank, loamy scents of decay
and we wondered what more could be done to a
battered shoreline already littered with shorn limbs,
haggard clumps of cord-grass and the distorted
detritus of a late summer's passing. But now,
the harbor's brine-bright and as still as glass;
its shallow waters calmed and warmed by sun
while fanned shells work their way back to
sediment and the sky shakes itself dry, pouring
torrents of blue down upon us as if the day's disarray
was little more than a set-to that had to be brushed
aside while all afflictions eased into air and life
went about the wearisome task of healing itself.

Tidal Ruin

Soon, when youth retreats
in the manner of the tides
supple shoulders drawing back from shore,
leaving behind nothing more
than spindrift and a tide-
line where all is bleached

with autumn's austere light. Watch
with fatigued and mournful eyes
the shoreline transform to gore
and the crueler allure
of salt's slow carnage, while skies
of communal gulls gladly grieve

and meandering winds carry their shrill cries
away from water towards heaven's door.

Abiding

I've come to this stretch of shoreline
with an uncertain purpose, watching
the early autumn light, like an over-
shirt cover the hillsides and the small
swells that rise then pause in dramatic
fashion, seeming to hold back time
and allowing me to draw in the soft,
mournful lapping of the waves and
to watch how the leaves, in the hushed
throttle of a morning wind, seem
suspended, too, in mid-flight as if
they've taken delight in their dying
before they fall like lurid pieces of
sediment and gather in layered ruin
beyond the tide-line, gravity and grieving
serving as sextant and compass, and
I'm wondering if you, who were born
beautiful and bound with grace, would
remember the profound emptiness of
this place and the life we had hoped for,
or the time we had stopped here some
years back, when you mentioned how
the light on its way to finding us was
but the final remains of distant stars
that had likely died centuries ago
before being swallowed whole by the
eager surf arriving with shattered
sprays of light, then slowly departing
with a muted drawl and hiss from shore.

III. The Heart and Hands

To love that well which thou must leave ere long.

—William Shakespeare

A Rural County in Connecticut

I prefer to wake in a place
such as this, when morning
air is marbled by mists and
the overlapping branches
of trees are bound in glister,
and a particular joy is found
in the tributes that come from
the throats of birds and then
finding a footpath leading down
to a field that appears to be
floating in light, bordered by
clusters of birch and low granite
walls, unperturbed by time
and blued with lichen, as if
the land knows the soul is in
need of this and would happily
keep it paddocked here while
the endless greens of summer
bleed into cider reds and flamboyant
yellows, fluttering or falling
in a rummaging wind, and,
knowing we die a little each
day, I've come to believe that
heaven is closer to us than not,
and that there's less difference
between what is and what
could be, and that it would
not be so difficult to spend
a second lifetime here.

The Blue Roofs, Rouen

—Paul Gauguin, 1884

I am drawn to the loneliness of this place,
and wondering if I could be happy here,
hidden away from a world where peace
and beauty still elude us, and take in
a diminished sky that continues to glaze
the delicate metal of each roof, so that
each appears rain glossed, drawing in
more shadow than light, and where
lampless houses lean into themselves,
keeping close communion with the earth,
offering up their small discoveries as
smoke from coal fires rise and tendril
in late autumn air and one can almost
hear the closing of misshapen doors
and the quiet unlatching of garden gates;
the melodic rumble of an oxcart traversing
the great hush of hillside, buckling away
from heaven, and where leafless trees
are pushed to the periphery making it
difficult to discern if this is the hour after
daybreak or the one just before the
deepening peace and meager light of dusk.

Awaiting Thrush

Day's last hour falls away and is dimly lit,
transforming the gardens into an exotic

landscape where branches are draped in violet.
House-bound porch is lamplit,

darkness uneasily settles and the quiet
drifts past and goes unharvested. Wet

leaves suddenly stir with a muffled sound
and there, just beyond

the hydrangea, a path of upturned stones
glisten like vernal pools and morning

glories convulse to tendril. Thinking the horned
moon might somehow coax from woodlands

the soft, mellifluent song of a hermit thrush;
instead, a catbird's screech from beneath a burning bush.

Inheritance

Wasn't it, though, a solemn
and peaceful place where walks
near day's end instilled a reawakening
of self and a certain wonder for the
smaller miracles of creation?
Though now, years later, silence
and sanctuary are both casualties
of progress and the curled tongues
and serrated fonds of budding ferns,
the pink pallor of mountain laurels,
and groves of river birch that had
settled sideways have all been
brushed aside by a wind as dark
as pitch, and even stars have been
pilfered from heaven and placed
upon a garish canvas of sodium
light and evening's vespers no
longer drip from branches to ear
like an unexpected grace but
from the cacophony of horns
and low-throttled engines and
the dull hum and crackle of currents
that scurry across these dark
deltas littered with poles and
wires that stretch out towards
the near horizon like misshaped
equations designed to measure
the expanse between the world
we had hoped for and what has
been salvaged and left to us.

Weeding Near Dusk

Midsummer and most living things
have forsaken sound or movement
and found refuge in the cooler air
settling in the long shadows that now
distance themselves from the house
as the afternoon's heavy heat weighs
upon the landscape and this after-
thought of a garden has made way
for more uninvited vagrants that
have bedded down and somehow
found sustenance besides the path-
ways of upheaved brick and the
amber spill of garden stone that
appears like a trail of cornmeal
in late-day light. One can only
envy their brute resilience as the
understory cools with the soft
purpling of higher air, perhaps
filling a larger emptiness some-
where beyond the born-broken
fence but before the nearby hills
falling away one from the other
in search of sleep and where a
wood thrush has taken refuge
from the dull, communal drone
of the bees and is offering up
its dreamy soliloquy of notes,
certain there's a sorrow deeply
rooted in every ending before
all begins anew except when
it doesn't and all the while
continuing to bear the pain of

these aging hands and knowing
full-well that ruin will prevail,
and so I choose to leave pieces
of my broken self and these
abiding weeds behind.

Prelude

—after Debussy's "Prelude to the Afternoon of a Faun"

It was the cascading scale
of wind-brushed chimes that
broke a silence as fragile as
porcelain and called to mind
the indolent descent of a flute's
first breath, slowly entering
the ear and receding into memory,
leaving to me this day—with
skies of weather-beaten blue
and a mending, mid-day light
that seemed to brush away
the dark and illuminate a foot-
worn path of sun-warmed stone—
where despair departs and
provides a reason for the soul
to envy the very weight and
frailty of flesh, much like
the faun, matted down in
the thicket, his heavy body
drowsy from the pungent
odors of honey-suckle and
wild grape, fluent eyes dim
with pleasure and deep in
dream, longing for the sweeter
abundance to be found in
a lilting sequence of notes
and a green, mellifluous sleep.

How Shall We Return?

How shall we return?
The hinge of oysters?
The glint in silt?
Salt's nomadic grit
that powders
autumn air and woodland fern?

Eyes will mourn
what dawn devours.
The quartz-bright gilt
of stars at night
once was ours
and now returns

to elemental form:
the nectar of flowers,
the delicate lilt
of summer light
as it pours
and softly burns

into dream. Careworn
and haggard, we forbear
though days are thick
with dew and silk-
soft mists that appear
without sound or touch or form.

Bonnard's *Almond Tree in Blossom* (1947)

Here, glory gathers in avian splendor, perched
upon branches where each lyrical blossom is
poised to soar in faint rustle, and where darkness
has been dreamt away as the world frees itself
from winter's cold, and hope, fully bloomed
and nearly whole, is rising up and set adrift
beneath a canopy of violet-blue air as day's
healing light repairs and restores a ripening
earth and neither the mortal eye nor the gilded
frame is able to contain this exquisite version
of heaven before us and the splendor of those
things we might throw our heart against and
lay claim to for a while—peace and color and beauty—
in what is, of all things, his final work of art.

A Want for Yellow

This is the type of day, bright as an
annunciation, that I will carry with me
and hold in warranty, watching the sun's
ribbons of light fold across the wooded
slopes and a small patch of land where
hills bottom out as geysers of forsythia
cascade into pools of jonquils, crocus
and tulips, and one could easily envision

how years could fall away and yellow
could progress beyond these simple
weeds and flowers and envelop all
of the world which is only fitting
for those things in life that are,
like warblers, both here and away,
and deftly blend the sky's ephemeral
blues with the verdant greens of earth,

and did I mention the patchwork
of cloud set high above the ridgeline,
infused with a flaxen shade I am
trying to recall before it struck:
rain-ravaged straw, piano keys
of ivory ambered with age or
the perverse hue of fingertips
indelibly stained by tobacco?

Cedars

—for father

The first time I lost sight of you,
you were newly orphaned and lying
in front of me tethered to a bed soon
after the cock-sure surgeons had stopped
your heart. Free of reprimands, your eyes

were fixed upon the futile beauty of day-old
flowers and the phantom shadows that fell
across pursed curtains, extinguishing all light,
followed by days that felt like the whole world
had fallen into darkness and ended. Years later,

after you passed, I went to visit a psychic near
Cambridge who claimed to speak on your behalf,
asking that I try to remember you as you were
before the pain of separation and the fatal fall
from self, and then, on my way home, recounting

those times I had failed you and certain that I would
grow old alone, I heard you, breathless still, pointing
out the improbable miracle of ancient, white cedars
rising towards heaven like wind-blown arrows scattered
across the ridgeline's bright anarchy of stone.

Sleeping Giant

A traprock mountain, located in southern New England, that anthropomorphically resembles a sleeping giant. The native Quinnipiac tribe referred to the mountain range as Hobomock or giant stone spirit.

As a child, I kept waiting for you
to rise from your deep, uneasy
sleep, dumbstruck and stumbling
towards a foreign sea just beyond
the edge of your long shadow, guided
by the oily light that sits upon the
waves, where I might watch you
draw down banks of clouds and
a sky of absentee blue closer to
the Sound and an astounded earth,
but still, like a fallen titan, you
remained transfixed, unable to rise
or wander, contemplating the silent
spectacle of constellations and the
stars and how the seasons seemed
to chase one after the other, deciphering
the language of ancestral gulls and
crows as groves of aromatic cedar
blossomed from thin sediment into
the sweeter air of spring, though now,
with days diminishing, I watch you
with tired eyes in early winter light,
and I see how you have been
summoned back into earth, raw
outcroppings dwindling with
each passing year, still limbless
and unable to separate yourself
from the near horizon, jaw

tightening and your body of basalt
diminishing and falling bit by bit
from the ridge line into these stark,
ragged canyons of ochre scree.

Garter Snake

It slept as a knotted snare doubled
upon itself before it was startled
and, like a narrow stream in wood-
land shade, poured itself through
the crevice of wall, slipping beneath
a phalanx of phlox and a bed of
crushed gravel. Divining tongue
led the dark ribbon of body towards
the mineral smells, sweet sap and
bright patter of water falling over
stone and a frantic slither carried
it as far as the middle of the road
before another type of sleep, wind-
combed, left its delicately plated
skin and its petal-pink mouth turned
skyward, as if it were a lotus blossom
drinking in the last rays of sun.

Hope Repurposed

In the abandoned courtyard,
a grove of olive trees in want
of water is gathering up the last
of afternoon shadow, green bleeding
to grey, limbs littered with spent
casings turning in a dejected wind
like pieces of worn tinsel, and
transfigured into feeders for the
great congregations of migrant
birds and, in the higher boughs,
tear-gas canisters set out as wind-
chimes seeking to make a sanctuary
of this space that might yet nourish
the soul and lend a voice to hope
in a grim landscape where everything
alive appears to be in mourning and
even an indifferent God must surely
find it all unsettling. Now, as day
unwinds, there remains only the
dim glow of lantern-light tethered
to lime-washed walls too broken
to repair, pimpled with the hollow
hurt of bullet holes that, curiously,
form the outline of a wingless bird,
inkblots of soot and a thin veneer
of dust while, in the distance, a
solitary scarf apes a red blossom
flailing haplessly in an acrid breeze.

Snow Leopard

I would fall just as far and hard
for you, having spent half a life
wandering among these desolate
slopes of blue-grey schist awaiting
the gift of a snowless horizon or
some sound other than vexing
winds or the muffled crumble
of loose stone sliding over
stone or even a life, with its
ample burdens, that does not
push so hard against me,

and where days are no longer
spent in stealth and shadow,
avoiding the predatory cold
and the sudden turns of weather,
but rather, awaiting those rare
moments when I am able to free
myself from the hold of a land
that's been eerily lifted, falling
in terrible tumult through weight-
less air with no ability to slow
my descent or to even roar.

Intrusion

The house is sleepwalking
again and we can hear it,
wooed by the moon, softly
wailing in the attic, primitive
planks and joists creaking,
and its head striking the collar
beam, moments before its
slow shuffle down the stairwell
where it gathers and warms
itself by the barrel stove before
continuing on down the narrow
hallways to contemplate the
ritual of living, knowing it
will outlive us, and awaits
our reimagined sleep. Then,
as night draws on, it alights
in slippered feet upon our
window-seat and, wanting
for beauty and perhaps a
landscape free of man,
whistles a mournful tune
that I can recall from
childhood followed by its
eerie endsay to the stars
and the dying wilderness.

Lines for Anthony Louis

What hurts most is the living and
the knowing that a furious life
could be so easily extinguished
and ladled into a section of earth
not much wider than a mail slot
tucked inside a sunken garden
that sheltered us from the haze
of a late-summer sun and where
ears could follow the church bell's
loud refrains between verses of
hushed amens and the trespass
of dry, thin-stemmed leaves
that scuttled past like so many
endings, though our dull hearts
and oppressed spirits were guided
from grief to gladness by your
sons and how comfort came in
the listening to decades strewn
with one-too-many wounds and
(how could it be otherwise?)
fewer healings and consolations
that youth fled so quickly from
your life and I caught myself
thinking that, despite our
differences, we were so very
much alike and now knowing
that your memory alone lives on
and how the service ended with
the salve of a small bird flitting
between windows wide with light,

having chosen that particular
moment to sing, unbidden,
past sorrow and all that had been
broken and worked its way to joy.

The Migrants, 1957

A weightless sadness lingers there
beneath the early autumn scatter
of exploding light, and the weary
sycamores, heat-hammered,
collapsing upon one another in
white-mottled grief; the dark drift
of weathered barns anchored near
furrowed fields falling out towards
the horizon like ruffles in a small
body of water. Presiding from a
porch, the foreman cannot possibly
see how eerily they call to us
beyond those catch-basin smiles
with stunted hands and lightless
eyes—the foreign flock annually
assembled in Sunday whites—
becalmed and bright with the
certain comfort of knowing, but
still not beholden to, a single place.
Tobacco leaves have been gathered,
hung and settled to sheds, and this
picnic pause comes a day before
moving on from fields of smoke-
soft nets to acres of apples and after-
noons upstate, perched upon thin-
railed ladders, carrying mottled red
and yellow bins into the sweet dank
of wet-stone basements while
twilight falls, and thoughts turn
back in reverence to radiant seas
of sugarcane ruffled by trade winds
and the healing light of home.

Hummingbird

Throbbing like a tiny
tribal drum, the bird's
an iridescent blur,
a lava-bright ember,
moving in an aerial
ballet from a state of
torpor to audible ash.
Easy to marvel at
its kernel of muscle,
size of a match-head,
wedged between the
scarlet chainmail warmly
lit, spreading across
its neck and the ink-
berry drizzle of wings,
as it rapidly rises from
its silken nest of hoar-
frost and dew-fall in
pursuit of the musty
scent of urns, where
it pauses, then flawlessly
retreats and ascends
without burden in
a rush of visible echo.

My Muse Is Slow Arriving

My muse is slow arriving, rooted in grief
and prone to lavish—just the way a plot
of open pasture, swaddled in shadow,
silently combusts when low clouds drift
apart, ushering in a flood of mid-day light;
other times, she'll rise in casual charm from
quiet waters before turning and spiraling back
to darkness or, more rarely still, she'll appear
in wind-blown dispatch, like a lone, nomadic
bird that returns to its northern-most range
when all things are still nestled waist-deep
in winter. Most endearing, though, are those
moments when I'll find her with head tipped
and mouth agape, content to gaze out upon
an open sea; take in the unearthly quiet of a
falling star; or, in half-sleep, retracing her steps
as fire-light expires and gives itself back to air.

House Finches

The small charm of migrants
has returned and with them
the making of another year's
nest tucked behind our wreath
of maiden-head fern and lemon
grass. There's no accounting
for how they keep the threads
of memory tucked within their
tiny heads, noting the seasons
that came and went, the quirky
ways of wind and terrain that's
a mixture of soft-tilled earth,
woodlands and pasture, and
then greeting us with their
incessant clattering as they
manically gather and build,
wanting only to create and
somehow extend life. Like
us, their work is slap-dash,
leaving a wrecked world of
fescue, feathers, silk and
soil and the falling apart
of day-long labors. And yet,
there's something about
their desperate labor and
frenetic motion even as they
forsake rest and reason,
defying gravity and coaxing
fledglings from a ramshackle
perch to blithely lunge and
assault the April air.

What Once Was Luminous

—for Michael Joseph

Sometimes memory will widen
and allow me to reach back
and retrieve pieces of my life
like how, decades ago, you

were the Oscar to my Felix,
the electric to my acoustic,
and how, in summer, we'd
gladly take up each day, walking

miles to meet in mid-morning light
past a landscape where we could
hear the earth breathing behind the
occasional fence-line or flatbed

flecked with rust, the wheel-less
cider mill and a smattering of haunted
barns leaning away from wind
to meet up with friends and the

chance encounter with adolescent girls
where so much and yet so very little
happened, and never knowing what,
precisely, we were all searching for,

though eventually you moved on
with certain steps and I was left
unsure what to make of that particular
hurt, while memory slowly dulled

the fellowship of us like those unfurling
fields of jeweled air I'd often pass on
my way home, slowly covering whatever
revelations remained in late-day shadow.

Mourning Dove

During these midday hours,
after weather has softened
and all sound and motion
seem to have abandoned
earth, the slender bird offers
up a wistful murmuring
from atop a split-rail fence,
as if its plaintive voice is
best suited to this time of day
when the very air is awash
in weariness, and the common-
place is slowly transformed
into a comely splendor of
stippled light, and all stands
exposed to those of us who
often find ourselves set apart
from—and unable to weather—
this broken world. Each phrase,
though, is like a wistful psalm
that deftly subtracts our pain
as it brushes past and seems
to slow time, giving way to
a sacred stillness where breath
holds as the bird flashes and
preens its shock of iridescence,
and then shudders off towards
some distant field in its soft
sail and whistling flight.

How Can You Mend a Broken Heart? (1971)

Because I was sixteen,
prone to sadness and in love
with loss, it was a question,
if we're being honest, I
was never eager to answer
knowing there is something
to be said about sadness and
the gift of grief and how it
settles deep inside the chest
and never truly leaves us,
and so, during that discomforting
time, I would dream hours
away without consolation
then gather up my high-school
heart, descend the stairwell,
close the door behind me
and take refuge with the
three oracles from Down
Under knowing the cost
of comfort would be an
exquisite hurt that could
only grow in the listening.

Moths

Brushed from evening's attic,
a profusion of powdered hues—
rain-softened green, citron
yellow and a dusky-gray bleeding
to blue—fluttering like clouds
of dust illuminated by the throw
of light, eager to expose their wings
and tiny contusions of body to the
black burst of bats or the fatigued
flame tucked behind a small
sanctuary of glass. They're like
young lovers returning again
and again, unable to wrench their
puddled bodies from light as if,
sulfur-struck, they'll soon ignite
in an embrace of mute sacrifice.
And yet, who among us has not
sought to make our way at night-
fall in long, unattended flights,
with appendages fashioned from
hope or anguish, in blind pursuit
of some bright yet fatal ending?

Bequeathed

—for Marianne

I leave to you,
my only daughter,
this wedding ring
of orange-blossom design,

golden-hued,
and etched by water,
its ornate engraving
weathered over time,

worn smooth
as ether,
blossoms dissolving
into something ill-defined,

like love, or some other
wound worth remembering.

Recess

Morning at last giving way to mid-
day hours when we descended onto
the schoolyard like a squabble of
greedy gulls in worn white shirts,
clip-on ties and plaid suspenders.
Solemn decorum of early morning
mass, with its luminous vernal pools
of stained glass, pasty amulets and
cleaving scents, now set by, we
worshipped, above all else, speed
and the ability to elude capture,
covering the tideless expanse of
asphalt as if they were on a slip-
stream to salvation or marveled
at older classmates who'd spread
their easy fictions of defiance
beneath the rusted awning of a
metal fire escape and tall, sun-
chafed windows, though we all
made do with simple joys, seeking
to out-run so much more than
banishment or a clumsy class-
mate until the hand-bell was
raised and shaken mid-air
like a loud sun and then we
trudged in glum procession
through the weathered doors
and up the lampless stairwell
to our desks that waited

for us like leg traps, some
of us having had our ears
or collars pulled on account
of our unkempt shirts, a
blood stain or the young
lives we had left untucked.

Magpie

—Claude Monet (1868)

Easy to overlook the bird,
perched on the edge of pasture,
taking in the land's transitory
splendor with its educated eye,
certain it would be difficult to
ask for anything more than this
still hour and soft settlement of
snow devoid of sound or
movement, where the boughs
of trees are angled and adorned
in sleeves of bridal white,
standing silent beneath a windless
sky that's been spun from frost
and clouds of angel-down and
all light flows and is held in
luminous shadows of diluted
blue and violet, evoking a kind
of fallen dusk that had ruptured
and then eased itself through
a wattle fence and a gate of
crusted ice where the pathway
leads to an unblemished
landscape—both small and still—
while the companionless bird
ministers to the solitude and
the exquisite spill of light.

Untethered

This time it's you
who's walking me back
from the ledge,
assuring me that no further harm
will come to those of us
who adore adagios, are prone to missteps
and are waiting for something other
than the buckling heart to break.
And I can see the glass canyons before me
are not so very different from
the ravine where earth ended and
I sought to calm *you*
before the frantic tremors,
the tightening of the chest
and then the sudden shrieks
falling upwards and passing us
soon after our tumble from a height
we could only have imagined
towards some distant dazzle of river
that had worn its way
in near silence
through rock walls and cluttered dams
of toppled timber;
watching rippled sheets of blue slate,
aglint with afternoon light,
slide together then,
just as easily, drift apart
like so many arrivals
and departures in a life.
Released from all earthly weight,

how remarkable our return then,
in a soft, twirl-tangle
of dust and wind and twine,
our corn-shocked bodies
ablaze and at last unhusked
and newly resurrected
uncertain of what, precisely,
had been displaced.

Buttermilk Falls

From this bare outcropping of stone,
I watch the giddy river flee its headwaters
beneath a canopy of hardwoods and
mountain laurel before it spools in languor
and seeks to separate itself from itself
within a wide platter of basin then pauses
as if weighing life beyond the ledge,
but unable to walk itself back, it succumbs
and tumbles forth, like muffled thunder,
into the lower chasm where it cleaves
the surface, rises rudderless and presses
on in hurried torrent, singing itself south
in liquid bluster, flowing away past saplings
and the tousled underbrush, bearing its
plunder of vivid fibers of moss-green
stubble and tablets of bark, softening
soil and stone as it feels its way forward,
wrinkling the landscape and staking its
claim upon the earth. The eyes can't
help but stop and settle there—though—
near the banks in the slow drowse of
foam and tea-stained water collecting
in oval eddies that work their way
towards—and then away from—one
another just the way the water manages
to gather itself before remembering its
path and then moving on to marry with
the astonished and witless what's-to-come.

Ash Wednesday

I meant to give you the gift
of tall Gothic windows struck
blind by sun, well-worn banisters
of polished mahogany adorning
stairwells of glazed stone, cobbled
courtyards and walls of brick dust,
hoping fate would be kind, only
to recoil from a wakeful sleep seeing
how time had long ago turned
and left, and that all of this had
drifted up and away from its
urban lattice into a brass-white
sky, leaving a cavity to be filled
in the smaller spaces floating
between blown out buildings—
the stale air littered with ash—
while a stream, dark as Lethe,
quietly flowed past, wind-wrinkled
water separating the worlds of
forgotten origins and ill-timed endings.

Whistler's *Nocturne in Black and Gold* (1875)

The subtleties which Whistler gave his pictures . . .
reveal his preoccupation with the lyrical and the literary.
—François Mathey

i.

All proceeds from some abstract abyss
between breakable light and darkness, where mists,
profuse and fathomless,
serve as backdrop to the easeful drift
of stars lifting from a forsaken earth
or falling, purged of sound, like a weighted breath.

ii.

Closer in, the shattered spray
of color and coal-smoke white;
the darker design and intricate way
drizzle dissipates in a summer's night
sky like airborne particles of frost
or ash that's smoldering and wind-tossed.

iii.

Day distant, this world will soon sleep
beneath a mottled sky of pewter
gray and lake-bed blue, while the slow sweep
of waveless waters,
shunting moonlight, push past
leaving but a faint, elegiac gleam of gold dust.

While Sleeping

—for Debra Ann

Waves are foam fraught and
licked white by an off-shore
wind, advancing then receding
in soft spools of convulsion,
like the cluster of blankets you
cradled last night, tangles
of hair pulled back as if
you were sailing head-long
into a gale. I watched you,
in luxurious retreat, closet
your heart from the day's
labors, exhausted with worry
and one-too-many obligations,
though, selfless even in
sleep, it seemed a small
smile appeared with each
deep breath as if you were
in the act of remembering
or giving something up.

Morning: Piazza di Spagna

—dedicated to Amy Clampitt

I suppose him in Rome, a body ruptured
and wild with grief, on a day that gives
rise to adoration and makes us thankful
for life and forgetful of our fall, wanting
to capture the beauty and promise of this
world and take in a morning sky of pear-
blossom pink and vellum blue and the
melodic chorus of birds clearing slumber
from their throats from somewhere beyond
the prattle of the piazza's fountain and

forgive me for wondering if he, in such
moments of fierce stillness, could see
how this city appears both a portal to
the past and the afterlife and has seamlessly
fused itself to one and the other or even
if he, in wakeful anguish, might have
considered the grandeur of clouds such
as these, saffron-splattered and illuminated
from within, hung high above the
paired towers like an opulent baptistery

of pearl placed so much closer to God
and so very different than the small,
cheerless room that still holds
pieces of his life where, specter-thin
and sick for home, he wished what
remained of himself out of his body
and the sad majesty of his final days
consumed with the distance between
this life's high requiem and the
louder silence he feared might follow.

Scenic Road

Connecticut has officially designated some 70 roads or highways as scenic.

Beauty's been abducted and taken
some place beyond the filling
station's exoskeletons of rusted
sedans and pick-up trucks that
have been assembled like brute
equations upon a lot of asphalt
and oil-slick stone, the window-
gated package stores abloom in
sodium light, and the moldering
planters festooned with sham daisies
and tulips that have been overrun
by a tangle of invasive weeds.
Even autumn-eager trees appear
distressed by something more
than drought, nursing deadfalls
while blighted evergreens and
abandoned homes fall back into
a dry, acidic earth. It's difficult to
find the scenic or the divine, though,
in a place that nurtures hurt and
where rain doesn't seem to wash
much away and where habitat has
been buried by haste and then eerily
exhumed, put aside and forgotten—
and where even a once ornate, slow-
to-rounding moon has been moth-
bitten, leaving behind a small
piece of itself in its pursuit
of some unfixed destination.

Musicien Français
(Claude Debussy)

Often solitary and aloof, he sought
the lavish and luminous with
works that often whispered in
their run to grace, and, some claimed,
to hear him play was to forget the
piano had hammers. But assuredly.
of all composers, he was the most
painter-like, using such terms as
arabesques, engravings, and *nocturnes*
with passages, given his predilection
for woodwinds and strings, he'd
want the listener to perceive and
not just hear; seeking to exploit
and reconcile, in the manner of
l'impressionniste, light and shadow,
tone and timbre, though it was
rumored he despised the label,
seeking refuge in a world one might
find between sleep and waking,
where clouds are endowed with
texture, fragrance has voice and
the sonorous spoils of the sea are
scattered beneath the tufted
slumber of a sun-dappled faun.

Why I Choose to Waken First

Because I know how much life
has already taken from you and
how difficult each night's descent
into sleep has been, while, eager
for refuge, you lie down beside me,
still trying to live with an other-
worldly pain and burrowed in
a heap of blankets that insulate
your body from the ache and frenzy
of this world, and how a few times
each night I waken to your fitful
dance with dream and the sound of
your breathing, rising and falling
in a dull, draped-in-cloud purr,
finding it near impossible to pull
away from the warm bond of
our bodies, as I rise before day-
break, dragging despair and
the past behind me, and prepare
the house for your solitary
arrival, ever mindful to breathe
deeply and pray before setting
aside the medicines and tea,
opening the threadbare curtains
and adjusting the window
frame in such a way that it
betrays the brighter bounty
of bird-song and helps to make

the endless expanse of blue
bearable, while allowing the
walls and what little is left
of the darkness to fall away
at least until the day I waken,
god-forsaken and heart-emptied,
to a life without you.

Edinburgh Nocturne

—for Michael Veve

Night comes on, loch-deep
and still, and the street's lamp-
light is muted by mists of low-
land grey that have taken the
angel's share of luster and left
a dim plume of halo encircling
us while somewhere, just with-
in earshot, I can hear tiny lances
of ice pelting earth and I find
myself thinking that even if I
wanted to expel my sorrows
they would surely find a safe
harbor here within the musty
closes of mottled stone that
lead to abrupt alleys and sun-
less streets where life and death
mingle and happily rise up
like a chorus, easily over-
whelming the heart, leaving
me slump-shouldered and dum-
fungled, resigned to darkness
and clumsily trying to forgive
myself and walk back time.

Evenfall

Certain that more than youth
is gone and will never return,
day finds us waving memory
back as clouds hastily spend
down the last of late autumn
light with no means to still
the air or prolong the flood
of color over color or the
moment between light and
dark when day dies back
and is nearly extinguished
and stars still keep to their
cold corridors like fragments
of ore in marl, and we quietly
gather with our infirmities
and settle near firelight behind
the broken latches of frosted
windows, as an indifferent
world turns dumbly on its
axis knowing there is so little
of the future left for us,
listening to the dull drone of
a skulking wind jostling branches,
kicking leaves and dreaming
our younger selves awake.

About the Author

John Muro is a resident of Connecticut and a lover of all things chocolate. He is a graduate of Trinity College, Wesleyan University, and the University of Connecticut. His professional career has been dedicated to conservation and environmental stewardship, and he has held several executive and volunteer positions in those fields. John considers himself fortunate to have worked at the Bushnell Memorial, the Hartford Stage Company, and the Wadsworth Atheneum (all in Hartford) early in his career, and his passion for art, music, and poetry remains to this day.

John has authored two other books of poems—*In the Lilac Hour* and *Pastoral Suite*—in 2020 and 2022, respectively. Both volumes were published by Antrim House and are available on Amazon. Since the publication of his first book in the fall of 2020, John has received several poetry awards, including a Grantchester Award in 2023. He has been thrice nominated for a Pushcart Prize, twice nominated for the Best of the Net Award, and his work has appeared in numerous national and international journals and anthologies.

John and his wife, Debra Ann, live on the Connecticut shoreline. They have four children and eleven grandchildren—to whom this book is dedicated.

www.ingramcontent.com/pod-product-compliance
Lightning Source LLC
Chambersburg PA
CBHW072153160426
43197CB00012B/2359